of European modernism was its radical commitment to "pure" abstraction. In a 1948 review of de Kooning's exhibition of black-and-white paintings, Greenberg hailed de Kooning as "an outright 'abstract' painter" who, in his desire for "purity," had rid his work of recognizable imagery and referential content to produce "an art that makes demands only on the optical imagination."[5] De Kooning disagreed with this formalist interpretation of his art, however:

> Painting isn't just a visual thing that reaches your retina—it's what is behind it and in it. I'm not interested in "abstracting" or taking things out or reducing painting to design, form, line, and color. I paint this way because I can keep putting more and more things in—drama, anger, pain, love, a figure, a horse, my ideas about space. Through your eyes it again becomes an emotion or an idea. It doesn't matter if it's different from mine as long as it comes from the painting which has its own integrity and intensity.[6]

And de Kooning, unlike most of the other major Abstract Expressionists (Pollock is the other notable exception), refused to devote himself exclusively to abstraction following his success as an abstract painter in the late 1940s. Instead, he began to paint in 1950 a series of expressionistic female figures, in defiance of Greenberg's belief that modern art inevitably advances from representation to abstraction.[7] For de Kooning, such a rule could only be seen as a limitation; such a rule was made to be broken. And in a Cold War era obsessed not only with aesthetic but also with social and political conformism, de Kooning's rejection of Greenberg's modernist orthodoxy and the artist's antisystematic aesthetic stance came to symbolize, in larger terms, a heroic commitment to personal freedom.[8]

De Kooning was born in Rotterdam, the Netherlands, and was apprenticed as a youth to a commercial art and decorating firm. He studied for eight years at the Rotterdam Academy of Fine Arts and Techniques, graduating as a certified artist and craftsman. In 1926, at the age of twenty-two, de Kooning sailed for the United States, a country he, like millions of immigrants before him, saw as a land of opportunity. Settling in New York in 1927, de Kooning supported himself as a commercial artist, house painter, and carpenter.

His friendship in the 1930s with the painters Stuart Davis, John Graham, and Arshile Gorky kindled de Kooning's ambition to become a modern painter. Davis, a talented Cubist and outspoken champion of modernism in New York, and Graham and Gorky, both immigrants from Eastern Europe, shared with de Kooning their sophisticated knowledge of Parisian modernism. In 1935 de Kooning spent a year on the Federal Art Project of the Works Progress Administration—a New Deal relief program for artists—and for the first time in his life he was able to devote himself completely to painting. A surviving sketch for an unexecuted WPA mural (fig. 1) reveals, in its combination of biomorphic forms and architectonic geometry, the young de Kooning's indebtedness to contemporary works by Gorky.[9]

However, in a series of paintings of male figures executed in the late 1930s and early 1940s, de Kooning began to assert his artistic independence. *Two Men Standing* (plate 1), featuring a pair of frontal figures with wide, staring eyes hovering against a backdrop of vaguely defined space, is related to Gorky's well-known images of himself with his mother.[10] But next to Gorky's pictures, in which the colors are bright and the contours firm, de Kooning's work appears

1. *Design for a Mural*. 1935. Gouache, 9⅜ × 14⅜". Stanford University Museum of Art, Stanford, California. Bequest of Dr. and Mrs. Harold C. Torbert

dark, troubled, and anxious. Painted in somber tones with ghostly outlines, de Kooning's men are anonymous, immobile, isolated; they stare out at the viewer with quiet intensity. Like the oppressed proletarians pictured by the Social Realists during the 1930s, but in a manner more subtle and psychologically profound, de Kooning's men embody the economic distress and pervasive melancholy of the Great Depression.

Two Men Standing demonstrates de Kooning's legendary inability to "finish" a picture—to seal it up in a state of polished perfection. Traces of process and revision remain everywhere visible on the canvas, and numerous anatomical areas that the artist found "impossible" remain unresolved. The hands of the man at the left disappear in a welter of nervous pentimenti, and his feet merge with the floor. The torso of the man on the right is fully modeled, but his legs are only faintly suggested and fade away below the knee, as if he were beginning to disappear. In about 1940, in the hope of attracting portrait commissions, de Kooning did manage to produce a few highly finished drawings (fig. 2), in emulation of Ingres, whose draftsmanship Graham and Gorky also greatly admired. But, chafing at the restraint required by such meticulous work, de Kooning abandoned this style after a handful of efforts.

Throughout the 1930s and early 1940s de Kooning, characteristically refusing to limit his options, painted both abstractions and figurative pictures; by the mid-1940s the two genres would merge (plates 3, 4, and 5). In *Queen of Hearts* (plate 2), one of several canvases of the early 1940s treating the subject of a seated woman, de Kooning assimilated the Synthetic Cubism of Pablo Picasso and Juan Gris, composing the woman's body of flat, detachable shapes, and positioning it within a shallow space defined by rectangular planes of color. The curvilinear forms of the woman play off the rectilinear forms of the background, and her body's warm hues—pink, orange, and yellow ochre—are set in relief by the surrounding cool greens.

Formally, *Queen of Hearts* is a successful, if somewhat static, Cubist painting. Psychologically, it is something more. Subtly anticipating de Kooning's famous *Women* of the early 1950s (plates 6 and 7), *Queen of Hearts* demonstrates a restrained yet insistent violence toward the female body. This violence manifests itself in the dissection of the woman's anatomy—arms separated from shoulders, hands missing, breasts rendered as detachable ovals—and in her craning neck and anxious, strained expression. In *Pink*

Angels (plate 3), the violence increases, as flesh-colored serpentine forms hurl themselves through space, twisting and writhing, lacerated by sharp lines of charcoal and cut by shards of yellow space. *Pink Angels* is a richly allusive painting: Its biomorphic figures are redolent of the fleshy nudes de Kooning admired by such Old Masters as Titian and Rubens, but call to mind as well the tortured bodies of Picasso's *Guernica*. Highly influential for de Kooning and other Abstract Expressionists in the 1940s, *Guernica* was Picasso's outraged artistic reaction to the atrocities of the Spanish Civil War. *Pink Angels* may be interpreted as de Kooning's more oblique response to the anxiety and carnage of World War II, which ended in the year he painted the picture.[11]

By 1946 de Kooning had moved, in a series of pictures executed in zinc white and black enamel, from Cubist and biomorphic figuration to biomorphic abstraction. Exhibited at the Charles Egan Gallery in 1948, his black-and-white abstractions were highly praised by avant-garde critics including Greenberg, and the largest of them, *Painting* (plate 4), was purchased by the New York Museum of Modern Art, helping to establish de Kooning's reputation as one of the leading abstract painters in America. De Kooning, however, did not conceive of the pictures as "pure" abstractions in the sense that Greenberg and others did. While *Painting*, like other works in the series, displays the marks of direct and spontaneous painting to a degree not seen previously in de Kooning's art—forms are roughly defined with loose, gestural brushwork; drips and spatters of enamel trip across the canvas surface—its highly irregular shapes do not read as nonreferential abstract elements, but suggest fruits, body parts, viscera, and furniture. "Even abstract shapes must have a likeness," said de Kooning.[12] Thus, even at its most abstract, de Kooning's art remains rooted in the artist's perception and experience of the world around him.

Most of the shapes in *Painting* are defined by white lines that cut into a black ground. The opposite is true of *Excavation* (plate 5), de Kooning's landmark canvas of 1950, in which tangled black lines slice agitated forms out of a creamy yellow field. De Kooning spent several months working on *Excavation*, painting, scraping down, and reworking the large canvas to produce a work of enormous power and complexity—a dense, seething, impacted field of slipping contours and open planes punctuated by sharp bursts of color and glimpses of anatomical and architectural fragments. Every inch of the canvas is charged with energy, and the canvas itself, loaded with writhing, muscular forms, seems to groan and almost buckle under the weight of de Kooning's ambition to produce an all-inclusive masterpiece.

Exhibited at the Venice Biennale in June 1950 and subsequently at the Museum of Modern Art and the Art Institute of Chicago, which purchased the painting, *Excavation* reinforced de Kooning's reputation as a leading abstract painter. But de Kooning was not content to keep mining the vein that his *Excavation* had opened, and immediately after completing the canvas he began to push himself in a new direction by returning to the subject of the seated female figure that had preoccupied him during the early 1940s. The major painting de Kooning began in 1950, *Woman I* (plate 6), absorbed almost eighteen months of obsessive effort. In the final version of *Woman I* de Kooning unleashed with full force the painterly energy that the complex structure of *Excava-*

tion had managed to contain. With a loaded brush and wide, splashy gestures, de Kooning described the looming form of a monstrous woman. Seated in the midst of a storm of pigment that invades her body from all directions, she stares out at the viewer with enormous, devouring eyes, her teeth bared in a threatening snarl. The woman's anatomy has been violently pulled apart and stretched across the picture plane. Her head is detached from her impossibly wide shoulders, her gargantuan breasts are flattened like giant pancakes, and her massive arms—shaped like legs in accordance with de Kooning's principle of "interchangeable anatomies"—are pulled away from her torso.

De Kooning's exhibition of *Woman I* and a number of related paintings and drawings at the Sidney Janis Gallery in March 1953 sent shock waves through the art world.[13] Conservative critics of the *Women* series complained of the pictorial chaos spawned by de Kooning's attempt to mix painterly abstraction and expressionist figuration. Radical champions of "advanced" art attacked de Kooning, previously known as a leading abstractionist, for his heretical return to the figure. Less doctrinaire critics, fascinated by the apparent psychological complexity of de Kooning's paintings, sought to interpret their meaning. To some interpreters, de Kooning's anonymous females suggested current stereotypes of American womanhood, ranging from the smiling "all-American girl" to the tough "big city dame," the mannish "new woman," and the smothering, middle-aged "mom." Other critics understood the *Women* in Jungian terms, as modern incarnations of archetypal feminine forces—primitive earth mothers, bloodthirsty archaic goddesses, awesome nature deities. Meanwhile, less exalted art-world gossip offered Freudian explanations: De Kooning's violent images of women revealed tensions in his relationship with his wife, Elaine (fig. 2), from whom he would separate a few years later; or the paintings exposed de Kooning's long-repressed fears of his domineering mother, who had terrorized him as a child.

De Kooning apparently conceived of the paintings as irreverent homages to the age-old tradition of the female nude in Western painting and sculpture. "The *Women*," said de Kooning, "had to do with the idea of the idol, the oracle,

2. *Portrait of Elaine*. c. 1940–1941. Pencil on paper, 12¼ × 11⅞".
Courtesy Allan Stone Gallery, New York

Kooning

ateforis

RIZZOLI ART SERIES

Series Editor: Norma Broude

Willem
de Kooning

(b.1904)

Art never seems to make me peaceful or pure. I always seem to be wrapped in the melodrama of vulgarity. I do not think of inside or outside—or of art in general—as a situation of comfort. . . . Some painters, including myself, do not care what chair they are sitting on. It does not even have to be a comfortable one. They are too nervous to find out where they ought to sit. They do not want to "sit in style." Rather, they have found that painting—any kind of painting, any style of painting—to be painting at all, in fact—is a way of living today, a style of living, so to speak. That is where the form of it lies.

Willem de Kooning, 1951[1]

FOR MANY YEARS Willem de Kooning was an avid reader of Søren Kierkegaard, the nineteenth-century Danish philosopher and founder of modern existentialism. Kierkegaard set himself against the German philosopher Georg Wilhelm Friedrich Hegel's "system"—a grand, pure, metaphysical attempt to understand every aspect of reality in terms of a dialectical process, involving a thesis, an antithesis, and lastly a synthesis that resolves and transcends the conflict between the first two. Kierkegaard objected to the facile ease with which Hegel's system resolved contradiction. Hegel could manage this resolution, said Kierkegaard, only by ignoring the ambiguity, confusion, and incompleteness that beset actual human existence. Rejecting Hegel's quest for general abstract laws, Kierkegaard focused instead on the conditions of the particular, concrete existence of the human individual—an existence that could never be explained objectively and only understood subjectively. De Kooning found in Kierkegaard ideas that were highly relevant to his own attitude toward art and life. De Kooning the painter, like Kierkegaard the philosopher, was opposed to any and all systems—which, in the case of art, meant sets of rules and regulations designed to govern the production of a painting or to explain the development of art history. "Art should *not* have to be a certain way," declared de Kooning. To rely on aesthetic formulas was to shirk the risk involved in authentic creativity: "I think it is the most bourgeois idea to think one can make a style beforehand. To desire to make a style is an apology for one's anxiety."[2] Thus de Kooning refused, throughout his career, the comfort of working in a preexisting style. Instead, he invented, moving restlessly through a succession of different styles that responded to and gave visual form to the ever-changing circumstances of his existence. Painting was, for de Kooning, "a way of living," inextricable from the ambiguous texture of his whole experience.

Because de Kooning's experience was constantly changing, his art was always in flux and in process. At certain times he would paint or draw recognizable figures; at others, he would delve into the abstract. Typically the modes would merge and intermingle, as de Kooning strove for an art that would be all-inclusive. His goal was to infuse his paintings with the greatest possible number of sensations and associations, ideas and memories, visions and emotions—all the while remaining open to further possibilities of mutation and interpretation. De Kooning's determination to remain in a state of openness and uncertainty manifested itself in a refusal ever to "finish" or perfect a painting. Typically, his art displays the marks of its making: fragmentary, disjointed, and ambiguous passages in de Kooning's works testify to the artist's continuous engagement in the struggle of creation.

To this struggle de Kooning brought an abiding awareness of earlier art, which was, for him, a source of constant inspiration. He expressed admiration for Neolithic fertility figures, Mesopotamian idols, and Pompeiian frescoes; he respected artists as disparate as Rembrandt and Paul Cézanne, Piet Mondrian and Alberto Giacometti, J.A.D. Ingres and Chaim Soutine. De Kooning was equally enamored of the "vulgar" imagery of American popular culture, purveyed in glossy magazines and tabloid newspapers, on highway billboards and Times Square movie screens. In youth and middle age he imbibed deeply the sights and sounds of lower Manhattan, soaking in the glare of neon and late-night cafeteria counters, studying the cracks in the pavement. In later years he absorbed the atmosphere of eastern Long Island, bicycling alongside the flat potato fields and watching from the shore the steely gray ocean. Over the course of his life as a painter, these experiences found their way into de Kooning's art, providing it with its content. But de Kooning's work was never illustrative, it was always allusive; "content," said de Kooning, "is a glimpse of something, an encounter like a flash."[3] And the ultimate meaning of each work remained, for the artist as for the viewer, elusive.

Standard histories of twentieth-century art identify de Kooning as an Abstract Expressionist, acknowledging the role he played in helping to establish the first internationally significant art movement of American origin.[4] Reacting against the provincialism of the Regionalist and Social Realist styles that dominated American art in the 1930s, de Kooning and his colleagues Arshile Gorky, Jackson Pollock, Lee Krasner, Clyfford Still, Mark Rothko, Barnett Newman, Adolph Gottlieb, Robert Motherwell, and Hans Hofmann explored and synthesized the major trends of European modernism—Cubism, Expressionism, and Surrealism—to arrive, by the late 1940s, at original and highly personal styles of abstract painting. Central to the aesthetics of Abstract Expressionism were a commitment to direct and passionate involvement with the process of painting and a tendency to produce mass images that spread across the surfaces of often monumentally scaled canvases, as in Pollock's dynamic poured abstractions, the expansive color fields of Still, Rothko, and Newman, and de Kooning's vigorous black-and-white paintings (plates 4 and 5). In works such as these, influential avant-garde critics such as Clement Greenberg, Thomas Hess, and Harold Rosenberg recognized decisive advances over modern European art. Soon they declared that New York, the birthplace of Abstract Expressionism, had replaced Paris as the capital of the modern art world.

Many observers, Greenberg chief among them, held that what made Abstract Expressionism superior to earlier forms and above all the hilariousness of it."[14] And for de Kooning, the *Women* also had to do with that icon of postwar American popular culture, the all-American girl—the beautiful, smiling young woman of cigarette ads and toothpaste commercials.[15] *Woman I*'s toothy snarl started out as a photographic cutout of the mouth of a smiling woman, clipped by de Kooning from a magazine advertisement and attached to his canvas as "something to hang onto."[16] Toothy grins and grimaces also feature prominently in many of the smaller paintings and drawings of women de Kooning made during and after his work on *Woman I*. In some cases, as in the right-hand figure of *Two Women* (fig. 3), the mouth is transposed to the pubic area, evoking the dread *vagina dentata* of male fantasy. The bug-eyed *Woman and Bicycle* (plate 7) has two lipsticked mouths; one she wears on her face and the other around her neck like a pearl choker.

Flowing out of the early critical responses to de Kooning's *Women*, de Kooning's own remarks about the pictures, and renewed encounters with the paintings themselves, a remarkable stream of analysis and commentary on the series by poets, artists, journalists, biographers, critics, curators, and art historians has continued unabated, making de Kooning's *Women* among the most interpreted paintings of the twentieth century. In a concerted effort to confer art-historical legitimacy on de Kooning's increasingly famous paintings, academically trained historians and museum curators in the 1970s and 1980s carefully traced the formal and iconographic sources of the *Women* to prehistoric fertility figures, Mesopotamian idols, Byzantine icons, and images of female nudes by such earlier masters as Rembrandt, Hals, Ingres, Manet, Cézanne, Kirchner, Soutine, and Picasso. And in order to demonstrate the historical importance of de Kooning's *Women* for later artistic developments, these scholars argued that de Kooning's involvement with the mass-media image of the smiling all-American girl had inspired the iconography of Pop artists Andy Warhol, James Rosenquist, and Tom Wesselmann. Parodies of de Kooning's *Women* painted by Peter Saul, Mel Ramos, and Robert Colescott in the 1970s made de Kooning's influence explicit, and served to reinforce the status of his *Women* as masterpieces of modernism. But during the same period the prestige accorded to de Kooning's *Women* was called into question by such feminist critics as Carol Duncan. Duncan charged that de Kooning, like Picasso and numerous other male modernists, had sought to affirm his own artistic and sexual liberation by painting female figures who were themselves monstrously distorted and less than fully human. Duncan argued that de Kooning's *Women* served to reinforce on a cultural level the social and sexual power that men assert over women under patriarchy.[17]

After five years of work on the *Women* paintings, de Kooning again moved away from figuration, painting in 1955 and 1956 a number of brash and vital abstractions that evoke the sights and sounds of the big city. The eight-foot-tall *Easter Monday* (plate 8), with its harsh tonalities, loud colors, and hectic brushwork, conjures up the dirt, noise, and energy of the streets of lower Manhattan. Scattered throughout the composition and adding to its visual interest are ghostly snatches of printer's ink, transferred accidentally from sheets of newspaper de Kooning had pressed over the painting-in-progress to keep certain areas from drying too quickly. Left in the final painting as a signifier of the urban

3. *Two Women*. 1952. Charcoal on paper, 22 × 29". Collection Robert and Jane Meyerhoff, Phoenix, Maryland

visual environment, the newsprint imagery enriches *Easter Monday*'s big-city aura and establishes a serendipitous art-historical link with Robert Rauschenberg's contemporaneous "combine paintings," whose clotted surfaces include actual sheets of newspaper.

In 1957 the congested energy of *Easter Monday* and other abstract urban paintings gave way to the broad sweep of de Kooning's abstract parkway landscapes. Based, in the artist's words, on "landscapes and highways and . . . the feeling of going to the city or coming from it,"[18] paintings such as *Ruth's Zowie* (plate 9) convey an impression of bold motion across open spaces. The wide swaths of paint, laid down with a house painter's brush, index de Kooning's thrusting, full-arm gestures and epitomize the vigorous 1950s style of "Action painting," of which de Kooning and his close friend Franz Kline were the leading exponents.

Calmer than the abstract parkway landscapes are de Kooning's abstract pastoral landscapes of the early 1960s, which feature larger, simpler areas of color, and a more intense and even light. Built mostly of luminous, close-valued patches of yellow, yellow green, tan, pink, and beige, *Rosy-Fingered Dawn at Louse Point* (plate 10) reads as a lambent, harmonious field; dark passages at the lower right corner and upper right edge add the only somber notes to an otherwise uniform brightness. *Rosy-Fingered Dawn at Louse Point* is one of the most peaceful and lyrical of de Kooning's paintings—a canvas steeped in the gentle ambience of eastern Long Island, where de Kooning summered during the 1950s before relocating there permanently in 1963.

Soon after establishing himself in his new Long Island environment de Kooning reintroduced the female figure into his art, inspired, in part, by the women he observed swimming, wading, sunbathing, and digging for clams on the local beaches. *Woman, Sag Harbor* (plate 11) is a florid, watery figure, floating in splashy ripples of hot pink, tomato red, and lemon yellow. Next to the *Women* of the 1950s, which seem to have been roughly carved out of paint, *Woman, Sag Harbor* appears softly modeled. But this is hardly a gentle image. The woman's body has been torn, stretched, and splayed across the picture surface, and the vivid red oil paints evoke flowing blood. Her vulva reads quite explicitly as a bloody gash, suggestive of menstrual bleeding and of de Kooning's association of the woman's pro-creative forces with the primal generative powers of the ocean waters in which she floats. Like countless male artists and writers before him who routinely depicted nude women in the landscape as bathers or sylvan nymphs, de Kooning identifies woman with nature and its life-giving forces. He defines woman in terms of her biological, reproductive capacity, while claiming for himself, as the painter of her image, the more exalted status as a creator of culture.[19]

By the late 1960s de Kooning was basing his paintings on a radical fusion of the colors and contours of female flesh with the imagery of surrounding water and foliage. With bodies, water, and plant life in flux, melting together in a messy mélange of pigment, *Two Figures in a Landscape* (plate 12) is barely legible as a representational image. The bodies of the figures—a small one, perhaps a child, at the upper left and a larger, apparently squatting one at the lower right—are defined solely by succulent smears of flesh-colored paint. Flesh becomes paint, and paint itself becomes de Kooning's primary subject—paint he has spread everywhere with sensuous abandon and allowed to run down the canvas in oily rivulets.

While continuing to draw and paint, de Kooning made a foray into sculpture between 1969 and 1974. Manipulating the clay with the same energy and directness with which he handled pigment, the artist modeled twenty-five different figurative pieces, which were then cast in bronze and other materials. Unconcerned with describing bone, muscle, or skin, de Kooning kneaded, twisted, gouged, and pummeled his clay, fashioning such lumpy, misshapen figures as the well-known *Clamdigger* (fig. 5). Although based on the artist's observation of men at Montauk standing in the shallow waters with their clam-digging tools, de Kooning's wobbly figure is barely readable as a contemporary worker, and indeed calls to mind more readily the hulking form of a primitive man, freshly emergent from the chaos of creation.

In 1975 de Kooning began a series of mostly untitled paintings that retain suggestive associations with landscape and seascape even as they approach complete abstraction. *Untitled XI* (plate 13) offers a disorderly riot of bold colors—reds, yellows, blues, and greens—set off against blacks, whites, and tans. The color is loosely handled and watery, spread and slathered with remarkable freedom, but to it de Kooning has added darker linear accents—some short and sharp, some loopy—that carve a wobbly design from the picture's free-flowing chromatic passages. *Untitled V* (plate 14) contains few such linear marks, but here de Kooning maintains pictorial order by placing a dominant patch of white set off from blue in the upper part of the canvas. This bracing white form, suggestive of sea spray against the blue of the ocean, provides a compositional focus, while efflorescent reds, yellows, and purples enliven the lower half of the painting.

In the 1980s, de Kooning's last decade of activity, the exuberant density and complexity of the late-1970s canvases gave way to increasing openness, simplicity, and refinement. *Pirate (Untitled II)* (plate 15) has a smooth, skinlike surface, the result of de Kooning's use of a wide spatula to spread on and scrape off the paint. Broad areas of creamy white and yellow fill the canvas with light; against them float denser strokes of red and sinuous lines of blue, red, and charcoal. Ghostly remnants of earlier paintings remain visible at the

4. *Clamdigger.* 1972. Bronze, 57½ × 24½ × 21". Whitney Museum of American Art, New York. Gift of Mrs. H. Gates Lloyd

margins of the canvas, creating a sense of depth and atmosphere and providing breathing room for the central pictorial elements. By the mid-1980s de Kooning had largely reduced his palette to the primary colors—red, yellow, and blue—laid down against a pure white ground. The gliding, ribbon-like strokes and fluent organic shapes in such paintings as *Untitled IV* (plate 16) gently echo de Kooning's biomorphic vocabulary of the late 1940s and frequently suggest as well the outlines of shoulders, elbows, breasts, thighs, and pelvic triangles so thoroughly explored in his earlier paintings and drawings of women.

In de Kooning's pictures of the mid-1980s we sense the painter's once-overpowering presence slowly fading from the canvas, leaving behind a trail of flamelike bands and patches of yellow, blue, and red—the basic elements of picture-making subsisting as a skeletal residue. By the end of the 1980s, de Kooning, stricken with Alzheimer's disease, had ceased to paint. His final paintings, sparse and ethereal, come as the surprisingly quiet denouement to a career that produced some of the most agitated and aggressive pictures of the twentieth century. But if de Kooning's last works are quiet, they still are not peaceful or pure. Their taut forms, subtly animated by a lingering nervous energy, loop and twist and glide, refusing to gather themselves into an ordered composition. No more than any of de Kooning's earlier pictures do these last canvases achieve stasis or closure. They remain open-ended, and so remain alive.

NOTES

1. Willem de Kooning, "What Abstract Art Means to Me" (1951), in Thomas B. Hess, *Willem de Kooning* (New York: The Museum of Modern Art, 1968), pp. 145–146.
2. De Kooning, "A Desperate View" (1949), in ibid., p. 15.
3. De Kooning, "Content Is a Glimpse" (1963), in ibid., p. 148.
4. The standard introduction to Abstract Expressionism is Irving Sandler, *The Triumph of American Painting: A History of Abstract Expressionism* (New York: Praeger, 1970). See also David Anfam, *Abstract Expressionism* (New York: Thames and Hudson, 1990); and Stephen Polcari, *Abstract Expressionism and the Modern Experience* (New York: Cambridge University Press, 1991).
5. Clement Greenberg, "Art," *Nation* 166 (April 24, 1948), p. 448.
6. Quoted in Aline B. Loucheim, "Six Abstractionists Defend Their Art," *New York Times Magazine* (January 21, 1951), p. 17.
7. See Clement Greenberg, "Towards a Newer Laocoon," *Partisan Review* 7 (July–August 1940), pp. 296–310. Reprinted in *Clement Greenberg: The Collected Essays and Criticism*, vol. 1, ed. John O'Brian (Chicago: University of Chicago Press, 1986).
8. On the relationship between Abstract Expressionism and Cold War politics, see Serge Guilbaut, *How New York Stole the Idea of Modern Art: Abstract Expressionism, Freedom, and the Cold War*, trans. Arthur Goldhammer (Chicago: University of Chicago Press, 1983), and the review by David Craven, "The Disappropriation of Abstract Expressionism," *Art History* 8 (December 1985), pp. 499–515.
9. For example, *Organization*, 1933–1936, National Gallery of Art, Washington, D.C.
10. First version, 1926–1929, Whitney Museum of American Art, New York; second version, c.1926–1942, National Gallery of Art, Washington, D.C.
11. Polcari, *Abstract Expressionism and the Modern Experience*, p. 274.
12. Quoted in Hess, *Willem de Kooning* (1968), p. 47.
13. For a detailed consideration of the critical response to de Kooning's *Women*, see David Cateforis, "Willem de Kooning's *Women* of the 1950s: A Critical History of Their Reception and Interpretation" (Ph.D. dissertation, Stanford University, 1991; Ann Arbor, Mich.: University Microfilms, 1992).
14. De Kooning, "Content Is a Glimpse," in Hess, *Willem de Kooning* (1968), p. 149.
15. This point is stressed repeatedly in the writings of de Kooning's chief critical supporter, Thomas Hess. See, for example, Thomas B. Hess, "De Kooning Paints a Picture," *Artnews* 52 (March 1953), pp. 30–33, 64–67.
16. De Kooning, "Content Is a Glimpse," in Hess, *Willem de Kooning* (1968), p. 149.
17. Carol Duncan, "The MoMA's Hot Mamas." *Art Journal* 48 (Summer 1989), pp. 171–178; reprinted in *The Expanding Discourse: Feminism and Art History*, eds. Norma Broude and Mary D. Garrard (New York: HarperCollins, 1992).
18. De Kooning, "Content Is a Glimpse," in Hess, *Willem de Kooning* (1968), p. 149.
19. See the classic essay by Sherry B. Ortner, "Is Female to Male as Nature Is to Culture?" in *Woman, Culture and Society*, eds. Michelle Zimbalist Rosaldo and Louise Lamphere (Stanford, Calif.: Stanford University Press, 1974), pp. 67–87. Related to this interpretation is Donald B. Kuspit's suggestion that "de Kooning impregnates and fertilizes the image of woman with his own artistic impulsiveness to give birth to her as the symbol of his own creative power." See Kuspit, "The Unveiling of Venus: de Kooning's Melodrama of Vulgarity," *Vanguard* 13 (September 1984), p. 22.

FURTHER READING

Berkson, Bill, and Rackstraw Downes, eds. "Willem de Kooning: On His Eighty-fifth Birthday." *Art Journal* 48 (Fall 1989), special issue.

Cateforis, David. "Willem de Kooning's *Women* of the 1950s: A Critical History of Their Reception and Interpretation." Ph.D. dissertation, Stanford University, 1991. Ann Arbor, Mich.: University Microfilms, 1992.

Cummings, Paul, Jörn Mekert, and Claire Stoullig. *Willem de Kooning: Drawings, Paintings, Sculpture*. New York: Whitney Museum of American Art, 1983.

de Wilde, Edy, and Carter Ratcliff. *Willem de Kooning: The North Atlantic Light 1960–1983*. Amsterdam: Stedelijk Museum, 1983.

Duncan, Carol. "The MoMA's Hot Mamas." *Art Journal* 48 (Summer 1989), pp. 171–178; reprinted in *The Expanding Discourse: Feminism and Art History*, eds. Norma Broude and Mary D. Garrard. New York: HarperCollins, 1992.

Gaugh, Harry F. *Willem de Kooning*. New York: Abbeville Press, 1983.

Hess, Thomas B. "De Kooning Paints a Picture." *Artnews* 52 (March 1953), pp. 30–33, 64–67.

———. *Willem de Kooning*. New York: George Braziller, 1959.

———. *Willem de Kooning*. New York: The Museum of Modern Art, 1968.

———. *Willem de Kooning Drawings*. Greenwich, Conn.: New York Graphic Society, 1972.

———. "Pinup and Icon." In *Woman as Sex Object: Studies in Erotic Art, 1730–1970*, eds. Thomas B. Hess and Linda Nochlin. New York: Newsweek Publishers, 1972.

Janis, Harriet, and Rudi Blesh. *De Kooning*. New York: Grove Press, 1960.

Kuspit, Donald B. "The Unveiling of Venus: De Kooning's Melodrama of Vulgarity." *Vanguard* 13 (September 1984), pp. 19–23.

Larson, Philip, and Peter Schjeldahl. *De Kooning Drawings/Sculptures*. Minneapolis: Walker Art Center; New York: E. P. Dutton, 1974.

Rosenberg, Harold "De Kooning: 'Painting Is a Way'" and "De Kooning: On the Borders of the Act." In Harold Rosenberg, *The Anxious Object: Art Today and Its Audience*. New York: Horizon Press, 1964.

———. "Interview with Willem de Kooning." *Artnews* 71 (September 1972), pp. 54–59.

———. *De Kooning*. New York: Harry N. Abrams, 1974.

Stuckey, Charles F. "Bill de Kooning and Joe Christmas." *Art in America* 68 (March 1980), pp. 66–79.

Waldman, Diane. *Willem de Kooning in East Hampton*. New York: Solomon R. Guggenheim Museum, 1978.

———. *Willem de Kooning*. New York: Harry N. Abrams, 1988.

Yard, Sally E. *Willem de Kooning: The First Twenty-six Years in New York, 1927–1952*. New York and London: Garland Publishing, Inc., 1986.

Zilczer, Judith, Lynne Cooke, and Susan Lake. *Willem de Kooning from the Hirshhorn Museum Collection*. Washington, D.C.: Hirshhorn Museum and Sculpture Garden; New York: Rizzoli, 1993.

First published in 1994 in the United States of America by
Rizzoli International Publications, Inc.
300 Park Avenue South
New York, New York 10010

Copyright © 1994 by Rizzoli International Publications, Inc.
Text copyright © 1994 by David Cateforis
All illustrations © 1994 Willem de Kooning/ARS, New York

Library of Congress Cataloging-in-Publication Data
Cateforis, David.
    Willem de Kooning / by David Cateforis.
        p.   cm. — (Rizzoli art series)
    Includes bibliographical references.
    ISBN 0-8478-1786-5
    1. De Kooning, Willem, 1904–   —Themes, motives.
2. De Kooning, Willem, 1904–   1. Title.   II. Series.
ND237.D334C38   1994
759.13—dc20   93-43141
                                                                CIP

Series Editor: Norma Broude
Series designed by José Conde/Bessas & Ackerman
Editor: Charles Miers; Assistant Editor: Cathryn Drake;
Photo research: Amelia Costigan; Compositor: Rose Scarpetis

Printed in Italy

Front cover: see colorplate 14

Index to Colorplates

1. *Two Men Standing*. c.1938. De Kooning's solemn men seem to combine features of the animate and the inanimate. Too poor to hire models during the 1930s, de Kooning got friends to pose for him, studied his own body in the mirror, or did sketches from a homemade manikin that he had dressed in his own clothes.

2. *Queen of Hearts*. 1943–1946. In the tradition of Ingres, Picasso, and Matisse, de Kooning in the early 1940s executed several paintings of three-quarter length seated women. *Queen of Hearts* is the most classically composed of these, but its smooth surfaces do not fully conceal the restlessness with which de Kooning worked and reworked the picture.

3. *Pink Angels*. 1945. Freely and rapidly drawn with little apparent premeditation, the writhing biomorphic figures and whiplash charcoal lines of *Pink Angels* testify to de Kooning's interest in the Surrealist principle of automatism, a technique of suppressing conscious control over the hand's movements as a means of producing unexpected and original pictorial forms.

4. *Painting*. 1948. De Kooning executed his famous series of black-and-white abstractions in zinc white oil paint and an inexpensive black enamel, Ripolin, familiar to the artist from his days as a professional house painter.

5. *Excavation*. 1950. De Kooning's quest to invest his art with the rich texture of his lived experience produced the agitated, densely layered *Excavation*. Shown at the Venice Biennale, the Museum of Modern Art, and the Art Institute of Chicago in 1950–1951, *Excavation* gained for de Kooning recognition as one of the country's leading abstract painters.

6. *Woman I*. 1950–1952. Numerous critics have seen in de Kooning's *Women* a combination of mid-twentieth-century urban vulgarity and the energies of ancient female deities. Of *Woman I* the critic Sidney Geist wrote in 1953, "Her image exists in the vast area between something scratched on the wall of a cave and something scratched on the wall of a urinal."

7. *Woman and Bicycle*. 1952–1953. Pin-ups and "girlie" calendars served as sources for de Kooning's 1950s *Women* paintings. *Woman and Bicycle* may have been inspired by the pin-up convention of a beautiful woman posed with a bicycle—an image associated with Lillian Russell in the 1890s and later re-created by Clara Bow in the 1920s and Marilyn Monroe in the 1950s.

8. *Easter Monday*. 1955–1956. With its impulsive gestural brushwork and raw abstract energy, *Easter Monday* epitomizes the style of "Action painting" pioneered by de Kooning and adopted by countless younger painters under his influence in the 1950s.

9. *Ruth's Zowie*. 1957. Several of de Kooning's abstract parkway landscapes, inspired by the artist's impressions of high-speed travel to and from New York, are named for specific towns or highways. *Ruth's Zowie*, however, owes its title to de Kooning's friend Ruth Kligman, who, upon seeing the finished canvas, exclaimed, "Zowie!"

10. *Rosy-Fingered Dawn at Louse Point*. 1963. From the late 1950s on, de Kooning favored for large paintings like *Rosy-Fingered Dawn at Louse Point* a nearly square canvas with dimensions in a ratio of 7:8. De Kooning took advantage of this format's inherent centrifugal energy, which pulls forms away from the center of the canvas and imparts a sense of dynamism to the composition.

11. *Woman, Sag Harbor*. 1964. Rouged lips and a toothy grimace float amid the puddles of red and pink paint that form the nude body of *Woman, Sag Harbor*. The unusually elongated format of the picture, which de Kooning painted on a wooden door, suggests a centerfold from a men's magazine that has been blown up to life-size.

12. *Two Figures in a Landscape*. 1967. De Kooning's representation of the melting bodies of *Two Figures in a Landscape* through the free application of juicy, flesh-colored pigment reminds us of his famous statement of 1950: "Flesh was the reason why oil painting was invented."

13. *Untitled XI*. 1975. The effulgent color and intricate painterliness of de Kooning's late 1970s abstractions make for a visual feast. *Untitled XI* combines broad passages of fluid color with snaky loops of dark calligraphy that wriggle across the canvas and keep the viewer's eye moving with them.

14. *Untitled V*. 1977. On his frequent bicycle rides along the coast of eastern Long Island, de Kooning absorbed impressions of the land and sea that found echoes in his abstract paintings. The splashy *Untitled V* suggests, through its color and composition, a windy blue ocean, white sea spray, and the dancing colors of a seaside flower garden.

15. *Pirate (Untitled II)*. 1981. In the 1980s, de Kooning began to paint by a subtractive method, dragging a spatula through thick masses of pigment to leave behind skinlike bands of color. To the smooth, scraped-down yellows, reds, and whites of *Pirate (Untitled II)*, de Kooning has added taut lines of blue, red, and charcoal, reminiscent of Arshile Gorky's linear biomorphs of the 1940s.

16. *Untitled IV*. 1986. The simplicity of de Kooning's late canvases, often painted in primary colors against a white ground, has reminded several critics of another Dutch-born modernist, Piet Mondrian. But de Kooning avoids the purity of Mondrian's rectilinear geometry, evoking instead through curving, sinuous lines the organic shapes of plant life and body parts.

1. *Two Men Standing.* c.1938. Oil on canvas, 61 × 45". The Metropolitan Museum of Art, New York.
From the collection of Thomas Hess; Rogers, Louis V. Bell, and Harris Brisbane Dick Funds and Joseph Pulitzer Bequest 1984 (1984.612)

2. Queen of Hearts. 1943–1946. Oil on charcoal on fiberboard, 46⅛ × 27⅞".
Hirshhorn Museum and Sculpture Garden, Smithsonian Institution, Washington, D.C. Gift of Joseph H. Hirshhorn Foundation. Photograph by Lee Stalsworth

3. *Pink Angels.* 1945. Oil on canvas, 52 × 40".
Frederick Weisman Company, Los Angeles

4. *Painting.* 1948. Enamel and oil on canvas, 42⅝ × 56⅞".
The Museum of Modern Art, New York. Purchase

5. *Excavation.* 1950. Oil on canvas, 80⅛ × 100⅛".
Photograph courtesy of the Art Institute of Chicago. Gift of Mr. and Mrs. Noah Goldowsky and Edgar Kaufmann Jr.; Mr. and Mrs. Frank G. Logan Prize Fund, 1952.1

6. *Woman I*. 1950–1952. Oil on canvas, 75⅞ × 58".
The Museum of Modern Art, New York. Purchase

7. *Woman and Bicycle.* 1952–1953. Oil on canvas, 76½ × 49".
Whitney Museum of American Art, New York. Photograph by Steven Sloman

8. *Easter Monday.* 1955–1956. Oil on canvas, 96¼ × 74".
The Metropolitan Museum of Art, New York. The Rogers Fund, 1956 (56.205.2)

9. *Ruth's Zowie.* 1957. Oil on canvas, 80¼ × 70¼". Collection of Thomas and Frances Dittmer, Chicago.
Photograph by Michael Tropea

10. *Rosy-Fingered Dawn at Louse Point.* 1963. Oil on canvas, 80⅛ × 70⅛".
Stedelijk Museum, Amsterdam

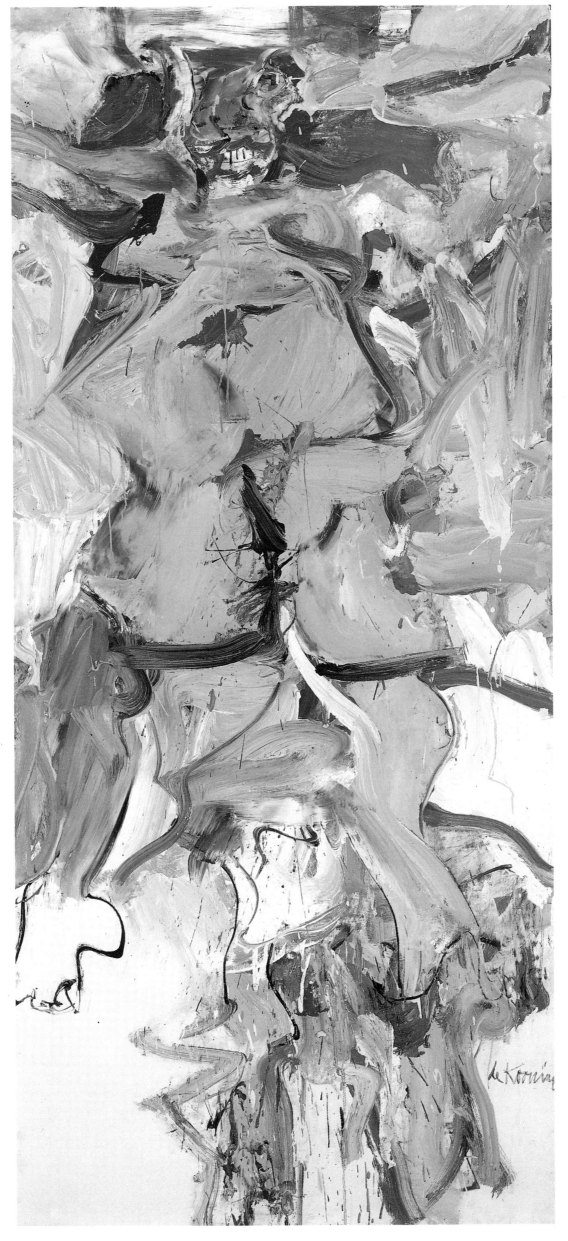

11. *Woman, Sag Harbor.* 1964. Oil and charcoal on wood, 80 × 36".
Hirshhorn Museum and Sculpture Garden, Smithsonian Institution, Washington, D.C. Gift of Joseph H. Hirshhorn Foundation

12. *Two Figures in a Landscape.* 1967. Oil on canvas. 70 × 80".
Stedelijk Museum, Amsterdam

13. *Untitled XI*. 1975. Oil on canvas, 77 × 88".
Photograph courtesy of the Art Institute of Chicago. Bequest of John J. Ireland; Joseph Winterbotham and David Aitken Fund, 1983.792

14. *Untitled V.* 1977. Oil on canvas, 79½ × 69¼".
Albright-Knox Art Gallery, Buffalo, New York. Gift of Seymour H. Knox, 1977

15. *Pirate (Untitled II)*. 1981. Oil on canvas, 88 × 76¾".
The Museum of Modern Art, New York. Sidney and Harriet Janis Collection Fund

16. *Untitled IV.* 1986. Oil on canvas. 88 × 77".
Collection of the Artist